Mother's are
Special.
They are the one true
Treasure on this
EARTH.

Enjoy this Day   Peggy + R.P.G.

© 2004 by Barbour Publishing, Inc.

ISBN 1-59310-000-0

Cover image © Photo Disc

Published by Humble Creek, P.O. Box 719, Uhrichsville, Ohio 44683

Printed in China.
5 4 3 2 1

LOVE LIVES HERE

The Heart of a Mother

JANICE CLARK

HUMBLECREEK
INSPIRATION FOR LIFE

A Mother's Love

A Mother's love is like a stream
That flows forever to the sea.
It never ends, because God sends
Replenishment abundantly.

Love's a strange commodity—
The more you give, the more you get.
Though you may try to drain it dry,
It's never been accomplished yet.

JANICE LEWIS CLARK, 1999

Many waters cannot quench love;
rivers cannot wash it away.
If one were to give all the wealth of his house for love,
it would be utterly scorned.

SONG OF SONGS 8:7

What Is a Mother?

Mothers come in all shapes, sizes, and colors. They may be young or old, pretty or plain, rich or poor, super-intelligent or barely getting by. Their religions, philosophies, and parenting styles may have nothing in common, but each seeks the best—as she sees it—for her children.

A mother may have carried her child for nine months "under her heart," or fought her way through reams of paperwork and other challenges to adopt. She may have acquired her children in various stages of growth as a "package deal" in a marriage, or taken in a child (relative or otherwise) in need of nurturing, or became mother to an adult through her son's or daughter's marriage.

Birth mother, adoptive mother, stepmother, foster mother, mother-in-law. The common denominator is love.

Love is patient, love is kind. It does not envy, it does not boast, it is not proud. It is not rude, it is not self-seeking, it is not easily angered, it keeps no record of wrongs. Love does not delight in evil but rejoices with the truth. It always protects, always trusts, always hopes, always perseveres. Love never fails.

1 CORINTHIANS 13:4–8

Your children are not your children.

They are the sons and daughters of Life's longing for itself.

They come through you but not from you,

And though they are with you,

    yet they belong not to you.

You may give them your love but

    not your thoughts.

For they have their own thoughts.

You may house their bodies but

    not their souls,

For their souls dwell in the house of tomorrow,

    which you cannot visit,

    not even in your dreams.

You may strive to be like them,

    but seek not to make them like you.

For life goes not backward nor tarries with yesterday.

KAHLIL GILBRAN, FROM *The Prophet*, 1923

Borrowed Children

Where are the children of yesteryear
Who filled my home with love and laughter?
Where are the faces I once held dear?
Gone, with their smiles still lingering after.

Those I was privileged to claim as my own
Stayed to grow up and are children no more.
Pinfeathers gone, they've fledged out and flown,
Leaving me here on the ground as they soar.

Others I shared for a month or a year:
Not mine by birth, but beloved all the same.
Though they have gone, there's a place for them here
In my heart, where so quickly they staked out a claim.

Every child's precious, a gift from above,
To nurture and cherish but never to keep.
Give each the best of your time and your love,
Guiding their waking and guarding their sleep.

Train them up gently, then let them fly free.
Urge them to try for the sky, for the sun.
Help each one grow to the best he can be,
For all are God's children; He loves every one.

Where are the children of yesteryear?
One moment here, the next they depart.
Vanished away in the mists of time,
Gone from my sight, but not from my heart.

JANICE LEWIS CLARK, 1997

Several years ago I read a comic strip in which the storyline was that a young couple, having tried for some time to have children of their own, had decided to adopt a child. The prospective mother was lying awake, tormenting herself with questions about what sort of mother she would be and whether she could adequately fulfill such a major commitment. Finally she faced the *big* question in her mind: *Can I really love someone who isn't my own flesh and blood?* At that point she looked over at her peacefully sleeping husband and had her answer. She smiled and went to sleep.

Tributes to
Mothers-in-Law

The tyrannical, hateful mother-in-law is a
fixture in our culture and the basis of many jokes. How often we forget that the beautiful words of Ruth were spoken not to her husband
or lover, but to her beloved mother-in-law, Naomi.

Intreat me not to leave thee, or to return from following after thee:
for whither thou goest, I will go; and where thou lodgest, I will lodge:
thy people shall be my people, and thy God, my God: Where thou diest,
will I die, and there will I be buried: the LORD do so to me, and more also,
if ought but death part thee and me.

RUTH 1:16–17 KJV

To My Mother

Because I feel that, in the Heavens above,
The angels, whispering to one another,
Can find, among their burning terms of love,
None so devotional as that of "Mother,"
Therefore by that dear name I long have called
   you:
You who are more than mother unto me,
And fill my heart of hearts, where Death
   installed you
In setting my Virginia's spirit free.

My mother—my own mother, who died early,
Was but the mother of myself; but you
Are mother to the one I loved so dearly,
And thus are dearer than the mother I knew
By that infinity with which my wife
Was dearer to my soul than its soul-life.

EDGAR ALLAN POE, 1849

What of that staple of fairytales, the wicked stepmother? It takes a lot of patience and prayer to make a "blended family" work, but it can be done.

Abraham Lincoln (1805–1865), whose birth mother died when he was only nine, was devoted to his stepmother. He wrote of her:

All that I am, or hope to be, I owe to my angel mother.
I remember my mother's prayers and they have always followed me.
They have clung to me all of my life.

Mothers are caretakers, homemakers, and much, much more.

She gets up while it is still dark; she provides food for her family. . . . She sets about her work vigorously; her arms are strong for her tasks. . . . She watches over the affairs of her household and does not eat the bread of idleness. Her children arise and call her blessed; her husband also, and he praises her.

PROVERBS 31:15, 17, 27–28

If the home is graced and sweetened with kindness and smiles, no matter how humble the abode, the heart will turn lovingly toward it from all the tumult of the world, and it will be the dearest spot beneath the circuit of the sun.

RICHARD A. WELLS, 1891

Moms

Wife, companion, sweetheart, friend,
One on whom we all depend,
Chauffeur, laundress, cook, and baker,
Casserole and cookie maker,
Seamstress, skilled in many arts,
Mending clothes and broken hearts,
Girl Scout leader, Sunday school teacher,
Confidante, advisor, preacher,
Bargain hunter, tutor, nurse,
Keeper of the family purse,
Neighbor, cousin, daughter, niece,
Making beds and making peace,
Always smiling, always giving,
What a busy life they're living,
Feeding children, dogs, and cats,
How do they wear so many hats?

JANICE LEWIS CLARK, 2000

Beware of Children Bearing Gifts

If you read the comic strips on a regular basis, you will notice a recurrent theme around Mother's Day. The children conspire to present Mom with a treat—usually breakfast in bed. They trash the kitchen and probably the bedroom and the rest of the house as well, but Mother is expected to accept her gift graciously and clean up the mess without complaint. After all, the traditional mother is always patient, understanding, and thrilled beyond all rationality with anything her little cherubs do. What kind of a mother would do or say anything to tarnish the shining gift presented by her adoring offspring?

And yet, isn't it also traditional to pass on the "mother's curse"? What mother has never been pushed to the point of intoning, "Just you wait. Someday you'll have children of your own, and they're going to be *just like you.*"

It wasn't Mother's Day, but the situation was similar:

Many years ago, when my older sons were four and six, the three of us moved from California to Washington. We were far from family and hadn't made any friends. I wasn't expecting any sort of celebration for my birthday, but the boys had other ideas.

I am definitely not a night person, and 2:00 A.M. is the absolutely deepest point of my sleep cycle. Naturally, that's when Jeff chose to wake me.

"Mama, I know we're not supposed to turn on the oven, but I wanted to make you a birthday cake. I don't know how hot to set it. Could you come and look? I'm sorry to wake you up."

I pried my eyes open and staggered down the stairs. An odor of vanilla drifted from the kitchen. Jeff kept up a steady monologue. "I put in butter and milk and sugar and an egg and some flour and baking powder and vanilla, and it tastes good, but we spilled some, and Jon stepped in it a little so it's kind of a mess. . . ."

Every square inch of my formerly shiny yellow kitchen was spattered with cream-colored cake batter. There were puddles on the table dripping onto the floor, splashes on the curtains, footprints across the floor. Jon was happily licking a wooden spoon; he had batter all over his pajamas, in his eyebrows, in his hair.

"Happy Birthday, Mama!"

How could I be angry with these sweet, smiling little boys who only wanted to make me a birthday cake? Oh, but I was. They had robbed me of my precious sleep, vandalized my kitchen, and broken a major safety rule by turning on the oven.

The best of intentions were no excuse for such outrageous behavior. I was so angry, I should have been breathing fire. I thought about spanking them, but I didn't dare; I'd probably inflict permanent damage. What I really, desperately wanted was to go back to bed and forget the whole thing, but I couldn't do that either, because the batter would probably set up like concrete overnight. So I mopped them off and sent them to bed, none too graciously, I'm afraid.

Jeff had set the oven at 200 degrees. The mixture in the pan looked close enough to a typical cake batter to work, so I

turned up the heat and proceeded to scrub the kitchen. By the time I was done, I had calmed down a bit, the cake was a beautiful golden brown, and the house smelled delicious. The boys were asleep, looking as innocent and angelic as sleeping children always do. *Thanks, guys,* I thought, as I wearily made my way back to bed.

The cake, by the way, was quite tasty, although a little heavy. Not too bad for a first effort by a little boy who couldn't yet read a recipe book. And the kids turned out okay too: both good cooks and both now parents themselves. I have passed on the "mother's curse" on numerous occasions and expect my grandchildren to carry on the legacy of keeping their parents from becoming bored and complacent. I'm sure they won't disappoint me.

Excerpt from *The Family Legacy or How I Survived the "Mother's Curse" and Lived to Pass It On* by Janice Lewis Clark

Laundry Musings

Little boys' pockets, full of odd things:
Bubble gum wrappers and butterfly wings
Nails, screws, and washers, a Crackerjack ring,
Pencils and pebbles and pieces of string.

The whole world is changing—each day
 something new
Cell phones and faxes and microwave stew,
Video movies and games on the set;
Grandma sends e-mail and cruises the net.

Satellites orbit, the shuttle's routine.
Holograms shimmer from each magazine.
Lasers for surgery, robot-built cars,
Telecommuting and photos from Mars.

Washers and dryers grow more automatic;
Glass fiber lines give us phones with less static.
Life is confusing, amusing but strange;
Isn't it grand that some things never change.

Little boys' pockets, full of odd things:
Bubble gum wrappers and butterfly wings
Nails, screws, and washers, a Crackerjack ring,
Pencils and pebbles and pieces of string.

JANICE LEWIS CLARK, 1998

the heart of a mother

Why Mothers Get Gray Hair

My youngest son is much taller than I. As a teenager, he found it amusing to look down on the top of my head and count the gray hairs. Now he tells me that he can't count that high. When he offered to pull the gray hairs for me, I told him to leave them alone, as I had earned every one of them raising him and his brothers and considered them in the same classification as combat ribbons.

Mothers are supposed to have nerves of steel. They should be able to handle any situation with equanimity. Just as one learns patience and faith by experiencing adversity, those iron nerves are the fruit of surviving many hair-raising (or hair-graying) experiences. Here's an example, from a letter written to my middle son on the occasion of his becoming a father.

For Jan, on your first Father's Day

To me, it was just a dusty garage. To a four-year-old with a propensity for climbing it must have looked like a jungle gym. That impish grin lit up your face as you literally ran up the walls and began to make rapid circuits of the rafters. It made me dizzy just to watch. My heart in my throat and my knees turning to water, I steeled myself and walked away, for fear my fear might cause you to fall.

It seems you were always just out of reach: out the window, on the roof, up a tree. You had no fear of falling; your fears were of another sort. Hiding within yourself, you avoided human contact; trees were safe, people were scary. Knowing personally the agonies of shyness, I tried to shield you until a wise friend pointed out that such "kindness" was ultimately destructive. "You'll cripple him. Let him grow."

$\mathcal{L}$ove LIVES HERE

It was harder, more terrifying, than watching you run the rafters. I had to stand back, even push a little, empathizing with the fear and pain but helpless to take it away. Inch by inch I prodded you out of the nest, until finally, to my astonishment and relief, you flew.

Now you are a proud parent, guardian and protector to an infant dancer who will all too soon be prancing on the rooftop. I see joy in this child, boundless energy, an inquisitive nature. You will find that parenthood is a constant balancing act, as you fight the internal battle between the instinct to protect and the knowledge that you must let go.

I pray that God will grant you the wisdom, and the endurance, to make the decisions that must be made and stay with them. I am proud and thankful that you have the advantage of an intelligent, courageous, and compassionate partner to "walk the tightrope" with you.

Love, Mom

JANICE LEWIS CLARK, 1996

The Hand That Rocks the Cradle

Blessings on the hand of women!
Angels guard its strength and grace,
In the palace, cottage, hovel,
Oh, no matter where the place;
Would that never storms assailed it,
Rainbows ever gently curled;
For the hand that rocks the cradle
Is the hand that rules the world.

Blessings on the hand of women!
Fathers, sons, and daughters cry,
And the sacred song is mingled
With the worship in the sky—
Mingles where no tempest darkens,
Rainbows evermore are hurled;
For the hand that rocks the cradle
Is the hand that rules the world.

WILLIAM ROSS WALLACE, 1819–1881

the heart of a mother

Tribute to My Mother

You can journey to Afghanistan,
Antarctica or Pakistan,
To Marrakech or other ports exotic.

You can travel on a stratojet,
A donkey cart, or better yet,
A camel, as you make this quest quixotic.

You can tunnel underneath the ground,
Or take a submarine around
The world (the schools of fishes are hypnotic).

You can take off in a rocket ship
To make an interstellar trip,
Surveying every galaxy sublime;

You can jump into your time machine
Go way back to the Pleistocene,
Or forward to the very end of time.

You can sift through all of history,
Mythology and fantasy
Or scan the web until you're ninety-nine,

But although you search with diligence,
Persistence and intelligence,
You'll never find a mother just like mine.

Janice Lewis Clark, 1997

Motherhood

Smiles and dimples, sweet delights;
Diapers, teething, sleepless nights.
Creeping, crawling, growing strong;
Into everything ere long.

Toddling, tripping down the halls;
Crayon murals on the walls.
"Mama," "Papa," happy laughter;
"No," "I hate you," follows after.

Bedtime stories, magic rings;
Skinned-up knees from slides and swings.
Halfway grown and off to school;
Teacher's smart but Mom's a fool.

Race through lessons, out the doors;
Messy room and half-done chores.
Plans and daydreams, fits and starts;
Broken bones and broken hearts.

Hitch your wagon to a star;
Need new clothes, some cash, the car.
Graduation, running wild;
All grown up but still a child.

Taste a bit of life and then,
Funny thing, Mom's smart again.
It's a calling like no other:
What a joy to be a mother!

JANICE LEWIS CLARK, 1996

A merry heart doeth good like a medicine.

PROVERBS 17:22 KJV

Train up a child in the way he should go: and when he is old, he will not depart from it.

PROVERBS 22:6 KJV

The mother's heart is the child's schoolroom.

HENRY WARD BEECHER, 1813–1887

The first and best school of politeness, as of character, is always the home, where woman is the teacher. The manners of society at large are but the reflex of the manners of our collective homes, neither better nor worse.

J. L. NICHOLS, 1896

Life: With Safety Net

Life is an ocean the sailor must cross
In a boat with threadbare sails:
Riding the billows from trough to crest,
Braving the fearsome gales.
And the waves roll up, and the waves roll down,
And the breakers roar and foam,
But the beacon light of a mother's love
Will guide the sailor home.

Life is a journey to faraway lands,
On a road fraught with perils and care,
Where many a beckoning dead-end trail
Awaits, the unwary to snare.
And the road climbs up, and the road slides
    down,
Over rocks and through valleys gray,
But my mother set me upon the path
With a map to guide my way.

Life is an acrobat's balancing act
On a narrow, raveling rope,
In a gusty wind, with slippery shoes,
And a tattered net for hope.
And the rope sways left, and the rope sways right,
And the watchers hoot and call,
But my mother's waiting with open arms
To catch me if I fall.

Though the sea is wide, and the road is long,
And the dancing tightrope sways,
Still I carry inside my mother's song,
That will last me all my days.

JANICE LEWIS CLARK, 2001

A mother who loves the Lord takes delight in passing on the teachings of the Bible.

Delightful task! to rear the tender thought,
To teach the young idea how to shoot,
To pour the fresh instruction o'er the mind,
To breathe the enliv'ning spirit, and to fix
The generous purpose in the glowing breast.

JAMES THOMSON, 1700–1748

The Scriptures teach us the best way of living, the noblest way of suffering, and the most comfortable way of dying.

JOHN FLAVEL, 1630–1691

My Mother

Who ran to help me when I fell
And would some pretty story tell,
Or kiss the part to make it well?
My mother.

Who taught my infant lips to pray,
To love God's holy word and day,
And walk in wisdom's pleasant way?
My mother.

ANN TAYLOR, 1782–1866

God pardons like a mother, who kisses the offense into ever-lasting forgetfulness.

HENRY WARD BEECHER, 1813–1887

Mama's Bible

Some kids are fond of history,
Adventure tales or mystery.
My favorite storybook was Mama's Bible.

Of all the heroes brave and bold
The films and comic books enfold,
None can compare to those in Mama's Bible.

And if a fella has a need
For good advice, why you can read
It all in Proverbs: that's in Mama's Bible.

Or if you're sad and feeling down
(There's always lots of that around)
There's hope and comfort all through Mama's
    Bible.

But if you're feeling good today
And haven't got the words to say
How great life is, try Psalms in Mama's Bible.

It's like a map or traveler's guide,
But better, 'cause there's love inside
And here's the best thing yet in Mama's Bible:

My Mama often read to me
How Jesus came to set me free.
There's wonderment and joy in Mama's Bible.

So though the book is old and worn
The leather cover bent and torn
All the world's gold can't buy my Mama's Bible.

JANICE LEWIS CLARK, 2002

the heart of a mother

At Our House

My mom is not a beauty queen
She doesn't wear high heels to clean
It's not a Beaver Cleaver scene
At our house

The house décor is mix and match
The furniture is old and scratched
So come on in—you can relax
At our house

No ladies come for bridge or tea
We don't dress up for company
We'll treat you just like family
At our house

No haute cuisine, no fancy food
No candlelight to set the mood
The meals are plain, but always good
At our house

My mom is not a socialite
In parties she takes no delight
She's home to tuck me in each night
At our house

My mom's a joy in every way
Her love and laughter fill each day
The neighbor kids all come to play
At our house

Janice Lewis Clark, 2003

Rock Me to Sleep

Backward, turn backward,
O Time, in your flight,
Make me a child again just for to-night!
Mother, come back from the echoless shore,
Take me again to your heart as of yore;
Kiss from my forehead the furrows of care,
Smooth the few silver threads out of my hair;
Over my slumbers your loving watch keep—
Rock me to sleep, Mother—rock me to sleep!

Over my heart, in the days that are flown,
No love like mother-love ever has shone;
No other worship abides and endures—
Faithful, unselfish, and patient like yours:
None like a mother can charm away pain
From the sick soul and the world-weary brain.
Slumber's soft calms o'er my heavy lids creep—
Rock me to sleep, Mother—rock me to sleep!

ELIZABETH AKERS ALLEN, 1832–1911